CANCER ON PURPOSE

CANCER ON PURPOSE

Michelle Jones

MICHELLE JONES

ISBN: 978-1-954755-38-3

Published by:
Restoration of the Breach without Borders
West Palm Beach, Florida 33407
restorativeauthor@gmail.com
Tele: (561) 388-2949

Cover Design by:
Andrene Campbell

Formatting and Publishing done by:
Leostone Morrison

CONTENT PAGE

Dedication

I am dedicating this book first and foremost in memory of my beloved sister Sonia Grant, who died in June 2003 from breast cancer, also to my other sister Sonia Riley, who is a breast cancer survivor.

Preface

The idea of writing this book came through the inspiration of the Holy Spirit. Since my childhood I have been hearing from God, sometimes through dreams, while meditating, and other times he speaks to me directly. When I was diagnosed with breast cancer in 2009, the Holy Spirit revealed to me that His name will be glorified through all this and that I will live to declare the works of the Lord. The Spirit directed me to write this book and entitle it *Cancer on Purpose*. The Holy Spirit also showed me that many people will be blessed by reading this book. This book was not a difficult one for me to write, because throughout my illness, I kept jotting down everything that was happening to me; I knew one day I would tell my story. I have written this book hoping that my experience and faith in God will help others who are battling cancer or any other illness, also to help others know that they are not alone and that with God all things are possible. God has created all of us for a purpose, and no matter how bad a situation seems, God can make it into something beautiful. As a child of God, all things will work together for your good because you love the Lord (Romans 8 vs 28).

Acknowledgment

First and foremost, I want to give thanks to the Almighty God, who is the true author of this book. God gave me the inspiration, and I could not have done it without His directions.

To my family and friends, thanks for everything. To my prayer partners, Erica Kelly, Debra Windette, and Wayne Pryce, you are awesome. I thank God for your daily prayers and fasting. May God continue to give you strength for the journey. Thanks a million, to my Holy Cross family. Thank you for all your support and encouragement. Heartfelt thanks to Moyesta Crumbie and Jennifer Williams. Thank you for being my tower of strength.

To my Bethel Church family, thank you for all your prayers and love. Sister Celie Anazodo, God bless you for all you do. Last but by no means least, thanks to my girlfriends Deise, Gretel, Carlean, and Kadiotou. You girls are my fan club. This book would not have been finished without you. God bless you all.

Introduction

Cancer is an illness that is feared by many people in our world today. When one hears the word "cancer," it is often viewed as a death sentence. No matter who you are, hearing the word "cancer" causes the mind to drift to thoughts that end with the worst prognosis. Am I going to die? How soon will I die? What is going to happen to my family? These are only a few of the many questions that come to mind. In this book, I will try to show you, with my testimony, how a bad illness such as cancer can bring about beautiful results. As a child of God, I believe that my father in heaven allowed me to go through this cancer journey for his divine purpose. I say this because we serve an omnipotent God who has the power to heal and deliver whomever he chooses and whenever he chooses. Isaiah 55 vs 8-9 states that "For my thoughts are not your thoughts, neither are your ways my ways. For as the heavens are higher than the earth, so are my ways higher than your ways, and my thoughts than your thoughts.

You may start thinking, how can this woman have cancer and purpose in the same sentence? But as you continue to read, I pray that the Holy Spirit will give you understanding, and I hope that you will be blessed. Cancer has killed many of our loved ones, and some of them also survived it. In this book I will share my experience with you about breast cancer and how I overcame it.

As I am writing this book, I had surgery six weeks ago, and God has healed me. No matter how life-threatening any disease is, as children of God, we are overcomers; and by his stripes, we were healed (1 Peter 2:24).

Nothing is impossible with God. God is the only one who has the power over life and death. He cares about everything that happens to you. For those of you who are not yet saved, I hope that my testimony will help you to come to know him. As for those who are already walking in his footsteps and are struggling with any form of illness, I hope you will be taken to another level in your

Christian walk. Jeremiah 29:11 (New International Version) states, "For I know the plans I have for you declares the Lord. Plans to prosper you and not harm you, plans to give you hope and a future." God bless you as you go with me through this journey.

My Life Before I was Diagnosed with Cancer

Named on Purpose

It all began in a small district called Orange Hill in the Island of Jamaica. In the year 1971, I was the seventh of eight children born to my mom. Without any thought that this name had any meaning, my mom named me Michelle. Michelle is the female version of Michael, meaning, "Who is like the Lord," or "Who resembles God." I believe I was named on purpose. This reminds me of Jeremiah 1:5, "Before I formed thee in the belly, I knew thee and before thou camest out of the womb I sanctified thee . . ."

I grew up in a large family where we just had enough to survive, but we went to church and trusted God for all our provisions. My mom and dad were not Christians at that time, but they believed in God and encouraged us to go to church. I was only twelve years old when I lost my father, he became ill and eventually died in his early forties. He was my superstar. It was the worst disaster that could have taken my family. I got very angry at God, for taking my father. At that point in my life all I could think is that my world has come to an end. I knew God was responsible for life and death,

11

so he had the answers I needed therefore I decided to seek him for answers.

Called on Purpose

For days I walked around that little house on the hilltop (my home) with my Bible in my hand seeking God for answers. I finally found him and became a Christian at age thirteen years. Jeremiah 29 vs 13 states that "You will seek me and find me when you seek me with all your heart" I found God and became a member of the Brown's Town Baptist Church. This was a Baptist church that was different from all other Baptists. I called it the Baptist Pentecostal Church of God. This church believed in the Holy Spirit, and we were taught about the gifts of the Holy Spirit, and there were members who had diverse gifts as mentioned in the Acts of the Apostles. There was always an event scheduled at my church seven days of the week.

There was this lady who was a member of this church who everyone referred to as a prophetess. Her name was Sister Marson. Many times she had visions from the Lord and messages for others from God, which would always come to past. Most of us as young people stayed away from this lady, because we didn't want God to reveal anything to her about us that we didn't want anyone else to know. I always kept my distance from her. Unfortunately for me, I didn't attend church one Sunday, and this lady came to my house to see me. That unforgettable Sunday, I looked through my window and saw her coming. I wanted to hide . . . All sort of thoughts started going through my mind.

What did I do now? Oh, God, what did you tell this woman about me? I walked nervously down the driveway to find out what this lady wanted from me, only to be told, "God sent me to you." My heart leaped; she opened her mouth and said, "Michelle, the Lord showed you to me in a vision last night and sent me to tell you that you are special, and he has called you for a purpose."

I was amazed and frightened. I asked her what she meant by that. She explained that he said he created me specially for his purpose, and I was not like every other little girl; he was going to use me for his divine purpose here on earth. I smiled, and she prayed with me and left. At that age I had no idea what God was going to do in my life, so I left it as it was said.

Prophetic Insights

Throughout my childhood I kept serving the Lord. God used me at school and in church to give exaltations. I had my first vision at age thirteen. God showed me an event that was going to take place at my school the next day, and I told my teacher and fellow students around me. No one believed me. They thought I was crazy, but it happened. They were all amazed. It happened exactly as I said it would. That was the first time I realized I had a special gift. I sometimes see things before it happens whether in a dream or vision. I grew up and pursued a career in nursing, and I then migrated to the USA in 2004 to be with my husband, where I am now living. The Lord continued to use me as a prophetess in my church. I would have visions of people that God wanted to bless or people going through difficult times, and God would send me with a message for them. I continued to work as a nurse, while God continued to use me for his purpose. God also instructed me to choose some people called prayer partners who would always keep me in their prayer daily, and oftentimes they would go on prayer and fasting for people whom God showed me needed help. I had four prayer partners whom God had chosen to cover me in prayer at all times. They have been very obedient to God's calling. They stood by me all the way and watched God used me and kept on their knees always in prayer, being obedient to 1 Thessalonians 5:17 by praying without ceasing.

Diagnosed with Breast Cancer

In December 2008, I felt two lumps in my right breast located at the upper part of my chest wall. I told my husband about it and decided that I would go to the doctor and check it out. I forgot about it, not thinking it could be anything serious. In February my husband reminded me, so I immediately called the doctor and made an appointment. After seeing the doctor, he sent me to do a mammogram, and of course, the mammogram looked suspicious, so they said they had to do a sonogram of my breast. After the sonogram they called a doctor at the radiology center who told me right there that there were calcifications all over my right breast, which appear to be cancerous, so they were going to contact my doctor immediately. My heart started beating rapidly, but I told myself that it won't be, because the devil would be stupid to try and attack a prophet of God in this way. I knew that all I had to do was ask my God to heal me. He had used me so many times to work in other people's lives, and I knew his power, so I knew this would be nothing for him to fix. I made preparation for a biopsy to be done. When I got the result of the biopsy, it revealed that I had cancer, and it was invasive, meaning it had spread all over my breast. A lymph node biopsy was not yet done, so no one was sure if it had spread to my lymph nodes.

I had a female surgeon whom my doctor had recommended. She explained to my husband and me that I will need chemotherapy and that they will be removing the right breast. Additionally, it was explained that I will also need radiation therapy because of the large mass. She gave me several referrals. Some were to radiologist, oncologists, and plastic surgeons. I received different request forms to have tests done for, e.g., PET CT scan, MRI, and the list goes on. This was a whole lot for my husband and me to ingest.

Sharing the News with Family and Friends

My mom was here in the USA visiting with me, so she was already aware. My son was only two years old, so I didn't have to explain anything to him. My daughter, fourteen years old, had just migrated four months ago to live with me in the USA. She was totally devastated and started crying and calling out to God asking

Him, "How can this be?" She just got the opportunity to be with her mom after so many years, and now God was going to take her.

She started calling everyone she knows that prays and asked them to start praying. I called home and informed my sisters and brothers; everyone was amazed. One of them commented, "Not Michelle, anyone else but Michelle." One of my sisters died in 2004 from breast cancer; she was only thirty-eight years old and left three children behind, so the family was not ready to accept another similar situation. Everyone started calling me and praying for me; one of my non-Christian sisters went to a church and got a prayer cloth for me to put over my breast daily. My youngest brother said no, God will not let her die. He said for the first time in his life he started kneeling several times during the night and prayed. He said, "Not Michelle. She is the one always serving the Lord from a young age. She is the one always singing for the Lord. She takes care of mom. God will not let her die, not now." When I informed my friends, some of them started crying, while others were praying like never before. For the first in my life, I heard all the good things people thought about me. Do you know that when some people think you are going to die, they start speaking the truth, whether it is good or bad? This is when you know exactly how loved or how hated you are. I went into my prayer corner, and I sought the Lord for myself. I cried out to my God. I said, "Lord, you must have a plan. I don't believe this is how you want me to die. I am only thirty-seven years old. Is this already the end of my purpose on earth." I reminded God how he called me when I was thirteen years old and told him I don't believe this is the end of it. I asked God what his purpose in this is, because I always saw myself as a "purpose" child. God has created all of us for a purpose, and all we need to do is to seek him for his purpose for our life.

My Prayer Partners

I called up my prayer partners and told them what the doctors said about the results and what their plan of care was for my recovery. We decided that it was time to storm heaven with our cries; we went on five days' prayer and fasting. As the word of God says, "Some things come only through prayer and fasting" (Mark 9:29). We cried out to God and asked, "What is this?" This is your purpose child, and what the doctors are saying doesn't sound like it's on purpose. We told God that we needed direction because we cannot face this on our own. My prayer partners were also praying for healing. After the five days of fasting and prayer was over, the spirit started speaking to me. I felt such peace like I had never felt before in my entire life. I said, "My goodness, this is the peace that the Bible talks about in Philippians 4:7, the peace that passeth all understanding." The spirit started to speak to me; as I continued to pray, God said, "My child, I am going to allow you to go through this for my purpose. I will not heal you just now. Go and read the chapter of Job. You shall not die from this cancer. This is to bring about my glory." It was so clear to me. I read the chapter of Job; he was a faithful man of God. Even though the devil afflicted his body with all kinds of diseases and took everything he had, he remained faithful to God, who rewarded him for his faithfulness. I called my prayer partners and told them what God said. So, we all decided that we have been trusting God for so long, and this time will be no different. We decided that we were going continue to seek God for further directions. We asked God to choose the doctors and the nurses. We placed the whole chemotherapy and other treatments in the hands of God, and we continued our "purpose" journey with God being the head; we sought him all the way.

God Continues to Speak

My oncologist told me that I will need to go through six cycles of chemotherapy. That means that every three weeks they would administer intravenous infusion of a mixture of cancer drugs. Every week I would get a drug called Herceptin, which I would need for a year because I have a HER2 positive gene. This gene causes cancer cells to grow quickly in my body, so this is a antiestrogen drug that I had to receive for a year. I was educated about hair loss and all the possible side effects of the chemotherapy drugs. I decided to just trust my God to take me through this.

One day, one of my friends called me, and she gave me a verse from the Bible, and the Lord told me that this verse would take me through this journey. The verse was Psalm 118:17, which states, "I shall not die but I shall live to declare the works of the Lord." That verse just stood out for me. God, who created me, wanted me to know that I would not die from cancer but that it will be a testimony for all to see. Each day I wake up, I kept speaking this verse until it become a part of me. Each time I went to church, I kept giving my testimony, and I shouted out loudly, "God said I shall not die from cancer." I kept telling my family members not to worry because I have heard from the Lord. "This is all on purpose," I said, "God's glory will be revealed through all of this." One day my sister Erica and faithful prayer partner in Florida called me, and she gave me this chapter to read, Psalm 34. She said the Lord gave her this chapter for me. When I got to verse 19 and 20, the Lord stopped me and told me that these two verses are the other two verses that will be my strength throughout this mission. The verses state, "Many are the afflictions of the righteous but the Lord seeth him through them all and not one of his bones are broken." I memorized these verses and read them in a different translation of the Bible so I could have clearer understanding. Again, God was telling me that I would go through a lot but, He would see me through, and no bone in my body would be broken. Each time I repeated these verses, I felt a new peace. God was with me and would continue to be with me through this whole thing. I told everyone that I am now ready to do my Father's will. Some thought I was in denial, some thought I was crazy, but there were the few who were already aware that when God starts using me, something awesome is about to happen.

Going Through Chemotherapy

Chemotherapy as known to all is treatment with cancer drugs or a group of drugs to help destroy or prevent the spread of cancer cells. Studies have shown

34

that sometimes it helps, and at other times it doesn't, but it is always worth a try by the cancer patient. These drugs usually destroy the bad cells in your body and, in the process, destroy some of your good cells. It also causes tumors to shrink, making surgery much easier. I was told by my surgeon and my oncologist that this chemotherapy was being given to me to shrink the tumor in preparation for mastectomy. These doctors had already planned to remove my right breast.

From my perspective, it was not their decision but God's; so, I just smiled, listened, and continued to be a good patient. I knew that my God was the only one who would make this decision. Being a nurse, I was knowledgeable of some of these subject matters. Through all of this, my dearest husband was right by my side. He is a very private individual, so you will notice I won't mention him much while I write this book. My prayer partners kept him in prayer all the way, so I know this young man was covered by God. I was scheduled to have six cycles of chemotherapy, one of which would be in three weeks.

First cycle of chemotherapy

All my treatment was done at the Maryland Oncology and Radiation Center, and my surgeries were done at Howard County General Hospital.

The first cycle commenced on the twelfth of February. My husband accompanied me to the oncology center. I went in with a very joyful temperament and was ready for my "purpose" journey. Then came the nurse that God chose to take care of me; her name was Alley. They gave me a combination of three chemo drugs: Carboplatin, Herceptin, and Taxotere. They inserted a port for the drug transport because my veins were not very prominent. The drugs were administered over a period of about four hours or less via intravenous infusion. I also had to take steroids and antinausea drugs to prevent certain side effects. I felt good for the first two days, but on the third day, I started to feel very sick. I was nauseous, and eventually I started vomiting; I have never vomited like that before. For the first time I felt like I was going to die. As my family watched me, I wanted to tell God just to take me, because I was ready to go to heaven. Looking at my mom's and fifteen-year-old daughter's face who was about to cry, I said, "No, God! Not yet, I have to make it a little longer, just for them. At that time, I forgot that I was on purpose for God. The feeling was too overwhelming. As the days went by, I was still feeling awful for about two weeks. I felt like I was always filled with fluid, very chesty, and yet my mouth was so dry. Most of the time if I was lying down, I had to use several pillows to keep my chest upward, because I would wake up choking; it felt like fluid was blocking my airway. There was one good week, and that was the week before the chemotherapy. I would feel like a normal person, and as soon as I feel normal, it was time to do chemotherapy again

Second cycle

It was three weeks already, and it was time to start the second cycle. This time my dearest sister Marita from my church came and sat with me while I was undergoing treatment. My friends were so supportive; they had booked my chemo days and decided when they would all come and sit with me during these difficult times. Each time I did chemo, I met someone new. The Lord would always bring someone in my path, who would just be blessed by talking with me. I realized that every time I opened my mouth, the spirit would speak through me. During my chemotherapy sessions, I met this lady who just loved my smile; she said there was just something special about my smile. A few days after this cycle, I ended up in the hospital with pyelonephritis. I was admitted for four days with severe pain in my lower abdomen. Throughout this time, I kept praying. God kept reminding me that this was on purpose, and his grace is sufficient to keep me. I had such joy and peace that I never knew possible in such time of suffering.

39

One of my colleagues from work came to see me, and she said, "Michelle, when I looked at you, you were just glowing." She said she could see God's glory all over me; God kept filling me with his glory and his peace.

The other cycles

I went through the other four cycles having the same side effects as before, except when I got to the fourth cycle, I felt like I was too sick to continue. When I visited the doctors' office, I was having shortness of breath. I told him I was too tired, I couldn't go on anymore and needed a break, so he decided to give me one-week break from the chemo. He sent me to the emergency room. As usual, they did all the tests they could and gave me some oxygen, and then found nothing wrong with me. Through it all, I maintained a positive outlook.

My colleagues from work kept calling me; they were all surprised because I remained positive. I would always tell them I am doing well despite how I felt physically, and I told them, "I shall not die, but I shall live to declare the works of the Lord." One of my colleagues asked me to meet with her pastor for prayer, because she thought I was in denial. She said she thought I needed help because I kept saying, "This cancer is on purpose, and I am God's servant fulfilling his purpose on earth." Everywhere I went people were blessed just listening to me share my experience. Even when I gave my testimony in church, people were blessed and lifted up just hearing me talk about God and what He was doing in my life.

As a child of God, one has to realize who he/she is in Christ. Your father is the one who can count every strand of hair on your head. He knows every small detail of your life; He created you, and before you were born, He planned your entire life. He Knew about your illness before it came, and that's why he said in his word by his stripes you were healed. Once you repent and commit your life to Him, you have to know your life is no longer yours. To live is Christ and to die is gain, which means whatever you do while you are alive, you do for the Lord, and when you die you go to the Lord. I kept living every day unto the Lord, and I continued to speak positively and have faith in God.

Mastectomy

It was now near the time for the doctors to remove my right breast; it felt a little scary, but I kept reminding myself that God is in total control, and He will not allow them to do anything to me that he didn't want done. I called up my prayer partners again, and we decided to go on prayer and fasting, as usual. We did this for two days, and I asked the Lord if it was his will for them to remove my breast and what did he want me to do at the time. On the day after the fasting, I picked up this book that a girl friend had given to me entitled *Healing*

43

Water Miracles. In the preface of this book, something caught my attention, and I read it over and over again. The book mentioned that sometimes God heals you directly, but sometimes he also uses medical intervention such as surgery to heal you. I said, "Lord, is this what you are telling me?" It became clearer and clearer to me. I prayed again and said, "God, can you give me a second answer." That same afternoon, I opened a gift basket that was given to me by one of my coworkers, and I saw a DVD that a colleague had given me that spoke about this lady who gives her testimony about overcoming cancer. When I played the DVD, the lady was talking about her experience with God and how she got mad and told God no, she didn't want breast cancer, and she wasn't ready to die. But God told her he wanted her to go through this for a purpose, and when it was time for her surgery, God told her he wanted her to have this surgery. This was my second confirmation about the surgery; this was just one day after prayer and fasting, and God had answered me twice. While spending more time with the Lord, the Holy spirit told me that after they remove my breast, they would not find any cancer cells anywhere in my body. I told my prayer partners and a few people around me, and then I prepared myself for the surgery. I even asked my doctors, "Are you sure you don't want to do a test before you do this surgery?" Both my surgeon and my oncologist said, "No, it doesn't make sense. The chemotherapy was just given to make surgery easier." I didn't argue. I just said OKAY. I knew they were not in charge; it was God, and so if He wants to stop them, He will. That is how powerful he is. I did this surgery in July, and after the surgery was over and they took out my lymph nodes to test, along with my breast tissues, they could not find any cancer cells anywhere — not in the lymph nodes, and not in the breast tissues. When my surgeon called me that day and told me, I told her that I knew and thanked her. I don't know what was going through her mind, but maybe nothing, because she doesn't know much about me or my beliefs. What I didn't tell her was that the Lord had revealed this to me. She was from a different religion; I didn't try to force my beliefs on her. Everybody was shocked with this result — the oncologist, radiologist, nurses, and family members

I just reminded them of what God told me, that "I shall not die from cancer, but I shall live to declare the works of the Lord." When God is present in your life, He always surprises everyone. "His ways are not our ways and His thoughts are not our thoughts" (Isaiah 55:8, 9).

Attempted Radiation

The doctors had planned to do radiation after the mastectomy; hence a month after the surgery, I had a visit with the radiologist. I had asked my surgeon if I still needed radiation; she said it was the radiologist's decision, but she would recommend it since my mass was so large. My oncologist told me the radiologist will have to make the decision; hence, when I visited the radiologist, I met a team of three who sat and spoke with me. They said the parameters that were there before to do the radiation is no longer there. However, they would recommend that I do it just to prevent a recurrence. The radiologist said if you were my sister, I would recommend that you do this. All these statements sounded so unsure to me. They also said they were amazed at this kind of result; it was not common, and my kind of treatment was a new kind of treatment. One member of the team said he was going to do research to see the outcome of patients with similar cases to mine. I decided it was time again to go on my knees in prayer. This act of God had confounded these people, and they were sounding strange; hence I told them I would do it and even signed the paper, but I was not comfortable; I had no peace. When you are a child of God, don't do anything that you are not at peace with. God promises to give you peace that passes all understanding according to Philippians 4:7. Based on that, the lack of peace would indicate that the pending decision was not within the will of God. I went home and discussed it with my family, then discussed it with my friends in the medical field. I said, "I don't think I need this." Nobody fought with me. Everyone seemed to agree with me. Anyway, I said God has been making all the decisions, so it's time to consult with him again. I called my prayer partners once more and prayed for God to continue to bless their faithful hearts. We went on two days' prayer and fasting, and I said, "Father, I am almost at the end of this thing, and if you don't want me to go any further, let me know." After the two days, I couldn't hear anything from God; a week passed, and I said, "God, what is going on? You are not answering me. I am getting worried. What do you want me to do?" I turned on the television and started to watch TBN, a Christian channel.

This pastor was in the middle of his sermon, and as I turned up the volume, he shouted, "Some of you have been praying to God asking him for answers and can't hear anything, but He said to tell you that He is folding His arms this time to see how strong your faith is in Him." My spirit leaped; immediately I knew God was talking to me; He said, "Michelle, I have allowed you to have the treatment all the way to this point. Now I want you to trust me that you don't need the radiation and that there will be no recurrence." I said, "Lord, not my will but thy will be done. You are the healing God. You created every cell in my body, and hence I leave you to do your thing." I called up my prayer partners and told them the answer. I

51

still had a small inch of doubt, so I asked the Lord to give me one more small reassurance. The spirit started speaking again, and the Lord reminded me of the word He gave me earlier about surgery. It was that he sometimes uses surgical intervention to heal us instead of directly. I said, "Thank you, Jesus!" Sometimes as Christians we are stubborn, but God does not give up on us; He knows it is our human nature to be afraid, but He always has a word to comfort us. Now I was sure of what I had to do, so I called the radiation center and told them I changed my mind, and I would not be undergoing radiation. I refused it. I am not telling anyone to refuse treatment. You have to be absolutely sure that God is talking to you, before you make such a decision. He created the doctors, and He gave them the expertise, but sometimes He has to remind mankind of who is in charge.

Attack from the Enemy

It has been a year now since I had chemotherapy. I went back to see my doctor for three monthly checkups, only to be called a few days later and be told that my CA-2729 level is elevated. When I heard that, my heart sank. I said, "Dear God, what is this?" When this level elevates, it usually means one thing: the cancer has returned, or there are active cancer cells in your body. I said this must be a dream, because God's name cannot be put to shame. This cancer cannot return; God would not allow it. I called up my prayer partners, and I informed them of the situation, and of course, we decide that it was time for prayer and fasting again. I was told by my doctor that I could wait three months and repeat the test or do a PET CT scan. I decided on the PET CT scan but couldn't get an appointment before one week's time. Well, at this point, I realized that God has given me time to fast and pray. We went into five days' prayer and fasting.

I cried out to God and said, "Father, this is not happening, because you have healed me. What will happen to my testimonies? Your name cannot be put to shame." I wept before God and asked him to transfuse me with the blood of Jesus so when the test is done, they will not find anything. I spent that whole week in the presence of God. I rebuked the devil every day and told him to flee from me, because I belong to God, and I am fulfilling His purpose here on earth, and my God's name will be glorified. Each day for those five days, I asked God to fill me with His Spirit and transfuse me with His blood; I had a glorious week in the Lord.

Of course, I did the PET CT, and it was negative: Praise God! The glory belongs to Him. This has just added another chapter to my book. The enemy has lost again, and God is victorious.

Purpose of this Cancer

<u>Testimonies from People Who Have Been</u>
<u>Blessed Through this Experience</u>

<u>Letter from Deise (coworker)</u>

Dear Michelle,

I just wanted to tell you that I am very proud of you. Not that you are a little girl and need reassurance, but what you went through with your diagnoses shows that one can go through cancer with dignity. This cancer never took hold of you, because of your faith in God and your personality. Instead, you took breast cancer out of the closets. I cannot pretend to know what you went through; however, I can watch it all in amazement. When you came back to work with that same engaging smile, you lit up my day. I knew you could do it. I just did not know that it would be done with such gracefulness.

I am so happy for you, for the journey you let us share, and for your miraculous recovery.

All praises to the Lord our God, who delivers us from evil and carries us through the valley of death.

You go, girl, still praying for you,
Deise Tome de Souza

Ibi's Testimony

When I heard that Michelle had breast cancer, I was so worried I called her to a room for us to pray. When we got to the room, I couldn't finish the prayer. I just broke down crying. The amazing thing is that she started praying for me that God should give me the strength he gave to her. She started encouraging me that God would heal her. I could see happiness in her face and the joy of the Lord all over her face. I loved speaking with her because it made me appreciate God more. Even in that situation she is still praising the Lord and believing in him; who am I to complain? I watched her every day through the whole process, still vibrant in the Lord. It has to be God that gave her the strength. The Lord has made her whole, and I glorify him for her. I pray that the joy of the Lord will always be her strength

Christine's Testimony

Knowing Michelle is one of the best things that happened to me as a Christian. In today's economy I have two jobs, mother of three beautiful children, and one child truly needs my time and attention. I thought this was quite a handful until one day Michelle came over to me while working. She whispered in my ear and asked me if I heard that she has breast cancer. Tears came to my eyes; but with a gentle and reassuring voice, Mish, as I called her, said to me, "It is okay, Christine. I have this cancer for a purpose, and I am going to be okay. Don't cry," she said to me, as if I was the one

60

with the cancer; I was amazed. Here is a young mother with such magnitude of pain, reassuring me in such a firm but calm voice. Michelle is a beautiful young lady, full of life and energy, always lending a helping hand at our workplace and always with a smile for everyone. She will give you jokes you will never forget for months. Sometimes I am driving, and I just remember her jokes and laugh out loud. Having always believed and trusted in the Lord, my faith grew stronger because I watched Mish go through chemo and surgeries, but she remained steadfast in her faith. Today my Mish is a cancer survivor, not just because of the medical treatment that was available to her or because of strong support from friends and family but mainly because of her faith in God. This has made her a living testimony to God's love and an

61

inspiration to me that with God, all things are possible. I love you, Mish.

My Daughter Jonelle's

Testimony

When I first heard about my mother being diagnosed with breast cancer, I was terrified. I started thinking about how my aunt had died from breast cancer a few years ago at the age of thirty-six and what it could do to my mom. The interesting thing about it is that I had just come to live in the USA with my mom about three months before she was diagnosed, and before I came two of my friends had lost their moms to cancer, so that made me feel even worse. I didn't know where to go and what to do or who to turn to, but I knew that God is always available. I decided to pray day after day and night after night. It was not easy seeing my mom going through chemotherapy. She suffered a lot, and it

63

was just one thing after another, but in all her suffering, she always put God first, and she is always saying, "Jonelle, I shall not die from cancer, but I shall live to declare the works of the Lord." I just kept praying because I knew that God wouldn't have brought me to the USA just to see my mother die. I started having my devotions in the mornings, praying and pleading to God for my mom. She went through chemotherapy and had surgery and is alive and well today, and it is all because of God's grace. This experience has brought me closer to God. I am now a Christian and walking with God and praising him every day for healing my mom.

64

God's Will

From the first day I was diagnosed with breast cancer, I knew God had a plan. I just didn't know what that plan was. As a child of God, I have committed my entire life to him, so I totally believe that he is in control. He promised in His word according to 1 Corinthians 10:13 that He will not give you more than you can bear. God just took away all the fear out of my life; I was not afraid of dying, because for me according to Philippians 1:21, to live is Christ and to die is gain. There comes a time when I just told the devil that he has lost the battle, because if I die, I will die in Christ; and if I live, I am living for God. That was the most powerful word that came to me. Fear is of the devil; Christians have no need to fear. The Bible tells us that we don't need to fear the one who can destroy the physical body but to fear the one who can destroy both body and soul. (Matthew 10:28): If we understand that all of us were created by God and he has a plan for our lives, then all we have to do is walk in His goodness and be obedient to His word, and He will take care of everything else

Each day as I went through the chemotherapy, God put a smile on my lips and a bubble of joy in my heart. Everywhere I went people kept telling me, "Oh, Michelle, there is something about you, despite all your sorrows and your pain. You just have this joy and this strength that is unusual." I knew it was God; He kept me going even when I could hardly make it. One lady at the oncology center always came to say hi, just to see my smile. She said something about my smile just lifts her spirit. God showed me favor everywhere, even at my workplace; he showed me favor with my coworkers and my boss. They supported me like they were my own family. They all came to my house to see me during my illness. Those who didn't bring gifts brought money. Even when I needed extra hours so I could stay home from work to get well, they gave me so many of their paid time-off hours; I had to refuse some. Even when I was hospitalized, God showed me so many favors with hospital staff and doctors; I was well taken care of.

God provided the best nanny anyone could have for my children. I never had to worry about my three-year-old son or my fifteen-year-old daughter. They were well taken care of. God provided money to pay all my bills; I didn't owe anyone for any long period of time. As the bills came, God provided the money to pay them. He said in His words if the birds of the air don't toil and he takes care of them, how much more will He take care of me, His child. Each day I stayed on my knees in prayer, and so many people everywhere were praying for me. The Catholics were lighting candles for me; those who worship Buddha were chanting prayers for me. The Muslims were praying for me; the Christians were praying for me. God brought so many groups together who went into prayer for me. God showed me favor by bringing all these lovely people into my life. My Bethel Church family kept me in their prayers, and as I went through my ordeal, I kept sharing the blessings of the Lord with them. I had joy and peace like never before in the midst of this cancer, because God was at the center of my life.

My Challenge to You

God has spoken to me and told me to write this book. He has revealed to me that this book is going to be a blessing to many. I am a woman of faith, and God has never failed me yet. I want to challenge everyone out there reading this book, whether you have been diagnosed with breast cancer or liver cancer or any cancer in your body, God is able. If you are HIV positive or you have been diagnosed with AIDS, God loves you. Whatever your situation is, my God is a healer. He said in his words that by His stripes we are healed. God sent His son Jesus Christ to die on the cross for mankind; therefore, we can always come to God with whatever problems we have, and He will meet you at your need. God heals HIV; there is nothing impossible for Him. If you confess with your mouth the Lord Jesus and believe in your heart that God has raised Jesus from the dead, you shall be saved. It is a simple prayer and start believing in the God that created you. A lot of people try to explain where we all come from, but God has placed in each of us a sense of Him. No matter how rich you are or how poor you are, when you look around you, you realize there has to be someone greater than you and me, who created this entire universe. Sometimes you might feel that there is something missing from your life; it is God talking to you. One day we all must die, but only God knows when and how. Don't be afraid of death or sickness; just leave everything to God. He is the Alpha and Omega; He is the beginning and the end. Trust Him today, and He will never fail you; it is simple faith in God. As the Bible says, if your faith is like a mustard seed, you can remove mountains. God bless you.

My Recipe for Overcoming Cancer or Any Disease

INGREDIENTS

- FASTING
- FAITH LIKE A MUSTARD SEED
- CONSTANT PRAYER
- THE WORD OF GOD
- OBEDIENCE TO GOD'S WORD

METHOD

1. Fast and pray for a day or two, or as the Spirit leads.
2. Read the word of God daily, especially the healing scriptures.
3. Walk in obedience to the word of God.

4. Believe what you have read and start speaking these words into your life.

5. Combine all five ingredients and allow the omnipotent, omnipresent, and omniscient God to do the rest.

About the Author

My name is Michelle Jones. I was born in the small Caribbean Island of Jamaica in 1971. I am married with two children. I have pursued a career in nursing and have specialized in obstetric nursing. I have lived in Jamaica for most of my life and migrated to the USA in 2004 to be with my husband, where I currently live and work.

CONTACT THE AUTHOR

I AM INVITING EVERYONE WHO READ THIS BOOK TO SHARE YOUR EXPERIENCE WITH ME BY LOGGING ON TO MY WEB SITE:

www.canceronpurpose.org

1. Communicate with the author.
2. Request prayer if needed.
3. Share about what you are going through.
4. Purchase copies of the book.
5. Give your comments.

Made in the USA
Columbia, SC
09 November 2022

70685186R00046